# SIMPLY YOU

### DAVID WESLEY ANDERSON

For my Mom and Dad—
they gave me these hands.

You were not simply
an artifact of my imagination,

You are not simply
a reason for my existence,

You will be the future
I hold—not so simply—
in my hands one day.

# THE
# DREAMS

These are the things
that hold us at night.

# EPHEMERAL

I whisper in pieces
for different places,
along moments passing by touches
pondering—
how beautiful you are.

Hot flashes of sunlight
rude awakenings that call your name,
ruffling sheets insinuating glances—
across the table.

No,
I believe I will be taking this route
through your heart,
the scenic one
where you can see everything
that I am doing.

There : is a calm sentimentality
space and intriguing mystery,
where play and hide seeks the touches of others.

Simply put and tangibly said,
dwindling straps baring wild life chests.

# QUINTESSENTIAL

How many days have your
stars danced around me,
played in the spaces of our hands wondering
when they will meet?

Meta : games we play on rainy days,
storms of hearts we are picked
apart naked : clothed,
in one another each inside around under.

Let unkempt and dazzle hang from your head,
twisting—kneading—petulant thoughts
pervade my imagination about you.

Aftertaste scents drag
near pearl endings,
where pleasure seeks company
with pleasure in soft whispers.

The circles of your elbows
have infinitely more edges
than this moment can elaborate.

# FOLLOW ME DARLING

Dearest you spark when I enter,
that smile of yours carries me right
over the edge of—your body is:
only an untouched path of delicacy,
stirring a whirl pool
of flame licking fingertips
and hidden soul traps.

In the case of your breath held
somewhere on a precipice wondering for more,
I felt a kind of astonishment simply as if
only a second took a stare to look
across from here to there,
where are those pretty eyes I missed?

Let us wind up and escalate
to somewhere new between one another,
both unwound from the night spiral—
to you trapped in between heartache and break,
a slalom of defeat a no win lose-lose,
just hold tight and hold on
as we let go.

# TWILIGHT'S FLICKER

Tell me why melting wicks tell
stories of our kiss,
dripping off
ears and
down necks—
circling chests?

Rain glass stylizes your outline
complimenting flickering shadows
that share a window with our eyes.

We are each a longing teacup
whispering to imbue our imprint on another,
hush quietly so they cannot hear
our evening's dare.

The following noon we shall draw
the swiftest pen to shade in our desire
with exacting pressure, borders
traced last night with a fine brush.

# A PEN FOR A LIGHT

I follow eyebrows to nose to
lips and teeth, to tongue on breath
on breath, to tongue in my lungs
w/o regret and
as the daylight burns
a slow burn between us—
bright embers say hello,
burn a slow friction between us.

For you (the only one) the mysterious one,
the one who threw away everything
for love,
for you I write—I pen my name
for every day is an exploration of your body,
of what is next from where
how much and
if I touch this what will happen?

I am but a torchlight for your darkness.

Don't fear fingers and let loose
what you have felt before,
we have much still to
touch when we
are alone.

# PERHAPS

If there was ever a chance for us
let us first be more sure of tonight—
than worry about the nights
that may never be.

If we lay still we can hear soft moans
over the living night,
reverberating—hesitating,
wishing to open wide our mouths
to the secrets we yet know.

If I let out my frustrations—
the infatuations, longings of what
was never and could not be,
would you hear them
as they ripple through your own stories?

If my fingers can trace your outline
clear as free flowing water, would
you believe that we are the same?

If we foretell the next twilight
before we lay twinkling with new stars
and imagined clouds—
illusive shapes, are we still broken dreamers?

# DELICIOUS UNCERTAINTY

My love I would say again—my love,
looking for that sparkle with a brush of hair—
my love, wake up it is morning once again.

May I search for your conclusions
the ones that draw near,
the ones that cause elastic to bare
to break little windows over here?

A flower bends along with the wind
the same as my fingers through your hair,
these are things that sting that are tender to play,
they start with you and end with tonight.

On toes—pirouette a revolt we watch in wonder.

If I reached that mirage
the one you have kept close,
the oasis only a sip of your insides
then on my way again.

# SO GOES THIS HEART

The black top knows your touch
in a stream of tears sun kissing,
so stretches road glory a
new destination for
this renegade heart.

Purple fire missiles
orange star bursts blue
spinning streamers strike,
stunning wonder in eyes—
we intersect in time.

We burn together within
twisting vibrant fires,
melt through stagnant air
drip down around thoughts,
a day more we will be together.

You bring me to that place of
yearning sliding love,
where we slip in silk and die
inside one another.

# ONLY YOURS TO TOUCH

Lose your fears in that feral moment
where we distinguish difference in others—
in us, the way we bend and blush
each of your echoes a paradise of words,
long soft strokes circular notions,
a velvet interlude where we protrude
lingo that you whisper when we play,
upright and then you say baby—
move me delicately.

Shown across a bare body pure
moonlight retreats to the neck,
she motions to come as
darkness illuminates her eyes,
though it seems when you stood over me
a section of the sky went missing
behind your penetrating eyes—
then I became only yours to touch.

Filling in holes someone else
dug inside of me,
painting away the scars
with kisses and laser beams,
just like you—we see.

# AT THE VERY LEAST

My love,
you are the tiniest fragment of this universe
and yet you have moved me
across the vastness of all the stars.

Chased by sun fire,
stumbling into velvet interludes
arms wrapped to keep back the flames
as you breathe easy under the smoke.

Beautiful shading out of time
from butterfly kisses
long slow neck missives that
reveal penned hopes and
dreams gone broke.

I like the way you smooth recline
and soothe my confines
in brushless fashion
contraindicating distractions
to focus solely on you.

In light of the gorgeous softness now seeping
through my veins, I find your darkness
intoxicating at the very least.

# WILL THEY BE ENOUGH?

One on the hand with eyes watching
you watching me past elbow—shoulder,
strap neck craned eyes rolling back.

My god, what eyes strike me
from you that dash my thoughts,
that take away any sense I might have had.

I'll trace limelight down necklines
past moan sighs past where you
thought hands linger
lunge tinker with needs—unspoken.

They don't know this,
the spaces between lines
that we fill with unending discord,
passionate swerving
bleeding dotted lines.

I'm not sure these hands could be words,
love covered in sin and scars
and wound stained bars tell me,
will they be enough?

# STEP STACCATO

Yes—you tore open sentiments
made love to how strange we were
waiting for subtleties
when what wanton needed was to striptease.

I know—you'd like lightning behind your eyes
a breathless grasping state,
an intently quiet loud arching release—I know.

We stand on a perilous
edge perceiving our passage
between us—as a wind bursts.

Hold on to me so every atom aligns,
here even magnetism finds love
between bonds and the stars watching above.

Baby blast me, say things that spit flames
dagger eyes and knives, I'd cut paths
to never cross you cut down me for you.

Let love continue stirring
our insatiable undesirable flesh,
together enmesh with a wondrous core
the simplicity of love making.

# WHEN I WAKE

With the sun opening your eyes
until the night beckons them to sleep
and even then—
I linger in twilight
holding you.

So in other words,
run with me to the edges of existence
until we collapse breathing heavily,
watching the rest of the sky move around us.

Lips and dreams and all manner of things
you let populate my mind postulating what if,
and the pendulum swings again in your favor.

The silence of your lips sways me into sleep,
just the kind of rapture I needed
after this long—
lonely day w/o you
to say hello.

As if you left a radiant remembrance
scorching my memory so as not to forget
the indelible place
you've laid upon my heart.

# MY SERENITY FLOWER

Even if we became ashes and bones
I hope that at least as we decay
our last molecules fuse together
to create something new.

You blossomed as a serenity flower,
waving to the wind of my chaos
unwind unearth
the land with my tornadoes.

May flowers bloom along your fingertips
when you reach for the stars,
where your dreams are still burning brightly.

We hid and found each other in shadows,
beds the rooms different
times different
lines we breathed into another
different but—the same intricate affair.

I desired not just a piece
or part of you—
but anything left,
after all you had been through
even ashes could love again.

# MY LITTLE PARTS

We flew
and broke the arrow of time,
caught between our lips pressing seconds apart
across infinity,
a waveform collapse.

They said you were ageless
with beauty breathed across eons,
but I wanted only this moment—
this minute,
not a thousand years to wait.

That wonderful brazen
carved along your lips,
sullen but brash where the lipstick
lines you smash my little parts—
melting me away.

# I WON'T BE CARELESS

Shall we play upon the face of the sun
where molten lines fragment others' dreams,
where pieces of them become part of us?

For you,
to get close to you
for you what is love,
we look for warmth
for you I built bridges of bamboo
swaying in the wind of your storms.

Will we ever feel that this is our natural
experience—two lingering souls,
broken with untold stories
on edges fated to fold?

I can only imagine a world left unexplored
you there left untouched,
unknown to anyone
to another's brush
of whisper or breath.

# LEAVE ME

I snake on your surface
meandering along points pointedly,
pressuring you to unveil a little more territory
for me to claim. Leave bites, not contrite nibbles
break depth inspire remembrance,
anticipate the drip of our feeding need.

Wind whipped we lay,
marks strewn eye and claw remain,
subject to mercy and heavy breathing.

You are something new,
something I've never laid eyes on before
laid with before,
became someone else with before,
before now.

# THE SPIDERS

These are the things
that shake our core.

# SPIDER'S STORY

Lines fingers swirls tips
like licks from fire that I pick off your lips,
small spaces that convey intimate faces—
warmth between fire lit toes,
where those pretty faces
see the entirety of body—but expressionless,
cast in black and white.

You can only see a piece of my story
tracing lines on hands along mouths
circling ponds hand in hand,
through a ray as in a keyhole
an outline shines in the prettiest form,
your body's silhouette.

Her lace display attracts conveys,
a wry smile made of silk, scarlet,
careful of the thorns.

# THE QUESTION

Sweet jingles wake—
tingling along my spine
itching down our synapses,
resting along the edge of your thigh
as if to say—good morning.

With a dark stripe led by nail tips,
I'd let you in under my skin but I'm afraid
you will show me something I've
never seen before, ruining another day.

Why can't I always wake up in a haze
wondering how beautiful you are,
as if this dreaming reality
finally coalesced, so cut back
through the punctuation—
it's another thing in between
each breath of ours.

Guide my hands along gentle waves
the kind that call from up ahead—
leading you down below.

Whatever that is left between us will be
on the sheets, the scents, and the pillow cases.

# PRETTY INTENTIONS

Fingertips wrapping hearts on hips,
some weave some sigh—another sigh
from you rolls through me like a freight train,
I wait wondering at the next station.

There is something about whispered curves,
delightful intentions that wake you up
and put you down—to the sheets that play
in our sandbox of melting ocean waves,
of sunsets and slow lightning.

You are fully formed figured and lush
looming over me, leaning into my mind—
making madness of my insides,
with pretty fragile things dangling on ears,
your ears, legs, wrists,
pretty little things wrapped in poison.

# INEVITABLY

You gaze with intent clearly and
inconceivably leading me
to where we both should go—
down into a fragment of the universe.

Each time a little death
one closer than the last,
we taste a bit of infinity
marking a transition through our lives.

You reawaken a new world of sensitivity,
pleasing satiating sensing melting my being,
a cascade of impulsive heartbeats and
how you extend and retract from my hands—
teasing me to come play in your spider web.

Unraveling in sights,
falling leaves—trembling knees,
there stands Medusa (you) in woven glory,
shredding me to unrecognizable pieces.

# POINTEDLY EXPECTING

Press in a way that stretches
and stays, that weaves what
you say into something that
unravels us both,
a swaying night's
rocking hips coaxed from raveled dreams,
lead me down circular pleasure paths.

Directionless but impress directly upon my
thoughts—where hemlines take us.

Every rippling moan to bare on thrust
competing wave lengths we don't discuss
how ten of my fingers hold you pretty,
such a pity for one night only.

Show me another sunrise and dine—
draw lace curtains just a bit of soul to bare,
water watches us only I find us leaning
into each other again.

# THE WRECK OF US

There again—
it strikes at me
a side glance of distracting misery,
impenetrable of course like
lace peering through a doorway.

I thought you would stay, not
tossed aside no bed post notches
just counting lashes, flickers, senses—
come hither my dear.

Trace bone to skin meet feelings within,
I would have you on the side in disguise,
head to toe would anyone ever know?

All I would be—flotsam,
you wrecked my ship
across the bow a mast lingers,
what have you now
but tattoos and scars?

Nodding along the beat with my thumb,
intent—contemptuous but open
to deviation, if proving our pleasure.

# WHAT COULD HAVE BEEN

Maybe if you succumb to the rainy
inhibitions plotting against
your window the sun will
come out and play, you
imagine a pretty thing on
a carousel swirling little
lies and the spider's
web does not thin.

But flames fanning translucent
waving delightful quivers,
I peek to realize you have
captured all of my sight.

Let scorching night melt
downriver between veins on
hands on legs on hands,
down necks and eyes beating wild.

These discreet ways—
things we could say,
subtle motions lost
between our footsteps.

# ANOTHER DESCENT

Imagine a warmth from
head to toe a blanket perspiring
but you don't care, your heart
beats faster and doesn't
notice—focusing
intently on this moment.

I cannot see
souls but your hands turn
me fuzzy, cause me to stretch
like spider legs which remind
me when you are no longer near.

A curious thing she comes
in surprise jumps into my hands,
sets new trains of thought and leaves—
like one daring night stand.

You became a spark of pursuit
nay exploration, another
adventurous curiosity.

In my oldest dreams we circled
each other young—
dared one another in tongues, time slowed.

# TALON

We come together prone to explosion
and rapturous atonement always
seems to elude our actions.

Far and away rumbling over hills
cast simply soft in velvet wheels,
silken sunsets eye lashes flicker,
a horizon curves around you.

I would be that brazen flash in your eye,
tickles down a spine clear cut hips
draw across our line,
accost in double time and again—
show me no mercy.

Maybe we are doing this wrong
wrapped in never—never land,
ignoring those enviously pious,
we are only about that
body and rolling eyes.

# FLOWER BLOSSOM EYES

Dilate at the fresh breath of morning
where jealous strands and silken
sheets know not of any difference
between us, lips and eyes magnify,
they stalk with ferocity every move,
strangled by a devilish scarf that
plays with stylized designs.

My love—you are all the terrible things
I want done to me, make me feel your rise
and subsequent ache when you leave,
I wish to trace elegant eclipses on chests,
this arching canvas where you swim
inside the fuzzy long strokes of carnality.

Show me little cicada, show
me how terrible you will be
burying into me
before you transform—a
succubus, chaining my taste forever
to the press of your fingers and slips.

# STALWART

She a sentinel binding your deepest
with wraps, thorns tipped in
poison knowing you are hers forever
in your wildest decay,
even a blissfully ignorant body
can be redeemed by the pulsing
waves of passion bound in lust.

A casual net already caught me closing in
on collars calling for closeness
but a corollary,
can we coexist with combined chaos?

I wait for your stab of sight,
whispering hair straps wrong
mingle and deceive me before I beg—
and you are on your knees.

Linger w/o regret
tomorrow brings a new fantasy,
another blue eyed wonder to chisel at your hips.

# REDUCTIONIST

Let us play—
simply children poking and running
twisting with fire,
yearning to break free from mortality
and for a time—we won.

From flicker to flame eyes
fire reflect kept indecency fanning,
these two candles
slowly melting into one set of bones.

Each morning the sun breathless
crawls over you,
regarded as divine window panes show
senseless sanguine, tear me apart with
finger bangs drip,
tell me there was no one else—
(it does not matter).

Whispering incandescent,
brush fine say hello
hair back strobe,
high lights pretty face
my love pretty,
secrets that dare live.

# CARESS ME

Wanton disregard—
how deeply your finger nails creep
leading me to bleed,
silence striking at midnight hearts
where thoughts linger on a cliff,
words on a moist tongue.

Forever in hearts uncovered by trust
concealed in shyness, kissing away fears
put hands where words once flowed,
show me what you mean to say.

Rolling shoulders tell no dirty tales
where mouths are kept shut by fear,
I miss your roar—your violent shifts into gear,
the rubbing pavement envious
and ice skating tires—
the slow world silent.

Phrase pirouette
a twirling flower—thorns lusting,
teasing touching
drifting through the mist.

# I'M OVER(COME)

Baby stretch the unrest
I'll unwind straps delicate traps
designed to pull me closer into your grasp.

Tonight and always linger next to me,
remind me when you are leaving but stay forever
when you arrive our actions blend together.

Let us define
down to the smallest bit each piece of
what we do when each are not near another.

I'm overcome with fresh red desire
you've left me haunted again
pacing moonlit avenues where we met
one night forever ago.

I'm locked inside the thoughts of you
of me dangling from lengths of you
spilling my need,
fervently requesting a formal release.

# BOUND IN SIGHT

I sense in delicate hands
a delicacy trapped in bends,
wraps of bands wondering for release
how your eyes they bleed to me. Together,
let us wake the darkness with our blistering
sight, our rampant bleeding emotion
our lustful hatred of anything not us.

At last we beckon the morning sun
glaring and jealous of us
delirious with sighs of yester night,
leftover pressures and lashes. You
strike me clear as day—lightning,
see a million words in eyes
that we shared w/o a sound.

You being peculiar
leaving me curious,
not wanting to leave you
leading me toward you,
I'm captured torn in delightful grasps.

We won't know each other
until the morning reveals what is left
of last night's descent through one another.

# THE
# SEAS

These are the things
that drown us.

# DEAR,

In my daze I see you clear as hypnosis
appear and there you go again,
out of reach but a hair I see waits for me.

Listen to my face w/o hands to distract—
clothes to interact and detach,
see eye to eye to eye to eye to clasp me.

Let little thoughts fall as pearls.

Even your sharpest ripe angles I can soften,
how playfully they push away others
but pull me closer.

Don't tempt me with wishful thinking,
the one who longs like a forest
to feel a breeze through her tired boughs.

I'd swallow you whole than a placebo
made of dreams come true—choke
on the bones of who you are now.

My love—where is your scent
the one that lingers decent,
wishing to descend?

# TELL ME

Are your lips ready
for the coming exhibition—honest,
I am teetering on edge
(exhilarating) waiting for a decision I wish
an act of divination
upon those starry eyes
peering out of your head,
free them into the night sky
where I will not be the only one to see.

Can we go on forever like this
placing our hands on these keys,
(the ones along our spine and chest)
toes to breast,
continue to play us softly when
nobody is there to sharpen my edges—
your rosy curves,
the ones that steal my eyes and
quicken my heart,
wrapping fingers in knots.

What will this night hold between us?

# KNOW-KNOW

When will the lilies dance
the skies laugh
the clouds smirk
and I collapse in a sea of violent roses
and blue daffodils?

Do you remember the first time lips parted
heads nodded
and arms sighed out in vain,
when a catalyst blew what you knew away?

Burn air bridges,
midnight sunlight quickening run,
heavy we are coming for each other
with trips up the sides of thighs,
insecurities illuminated in eyes.

But be : you that someone in : side,
wild eyed pretentious
curious apprehensive,
know : no boundary nor horizon.

# A SHORT WHILE

Rosy cheeks speak to me
downwind road—
touching night's arms
a street lamp lights way.

I lay between your words—
a soft breathless haven,
eyes closed listening to
your chest skimming heat.

Oh—madness while you roam
a short while linger, please.

Every sight a photo imprints
upon me a perpetual ache
untouchable only by you,
magic in distant fingers
breathing to draw back
upon our cedar bow.

We take deep strokes [gulfs]
in the broad moonlight,
one another over under a lake bed—
a strobe of lens flare (f)lashes.

# THE WATERFALL

Eyes shade shifting light
Summer through September,
sipping hair Spring remember
copper sky above down her neck
November, the point w/o return—
bliss nothing hiding fantasizing
let me slip inside that thing you hide,
the one behind your closed hands so
we can do away with sweet serenades,
let us bring the honest emotion
one and done devotion in pretty fingers,
lingering below your slopes fall—
into you over again a somber thought
trip alone, step over onto with you
and this tragedy of us begins and ends,
a circular sensual solitary confinement
where graceful water runs beside—we
ride, gesticulating incantations
smooth rhythmic excitations,
(lullabies) poured over a
pair of warm souls.

# LISTEN TO YOUR HEART

Beating in cadence to a quiet love
a wrapped
cushioned fiery love,
a wondrous
blooming desirous love.

Intentions and our comprehension mixed
into a kissable abyss that was lost in the
headlights
of other cars that night.

In the night's shadow we delight
in pre-twilight songs that swim,
in our chests that swirl
in our hearts that hold us
close against the cold.

Numerous stories between us in sheets
in cars under candles lit like last night
in rain under skies blue,
gray green stars.

# AN EPODE TO YOU

My love you should breathe—for
we spent this unquiet afternoon flying
in spaces we made between the sheets, flowers.

You are the unpicked string waiting to strum
wound tight thinking pluck me quickly now
with that wet look, my demise
singing from eyes—I like your scars.

Dreams of Summer still linger to poke
holes in my new attempts at understanding—
winter, I'm left a frozen look.

These were nights when time left us alone,
when we pressed play when we never woke,
when we were infinite—we were young.

Are you the one swirling as I in circles
falling in heaps of hay,
where unkempt soft tests our fall tonight?

# KALEIDOSCOPE

Last chance to self-destruct,
to show me the real you—
impenetrable escalating,
the one with
fire in her eyes
and lava flooding veins.

When we woke finally we
scattered bones,
covering what we did
to one another in a fit of red tension,
rose thorns around scars
that bared bright against night.

You swirl in wind teasing leaves,
spinning them with the sun—clouds
dance above (smile),
through the rays
letting light close our wounds.

Long before you came my eyes
were already closed, wavelike ripples
dug my back—a reminder for the
silence to keep beating.

# AS THE MOON TURNS

Can you shift us into twisting night,
following headlights like fingers
trailing our thoughts?

Let us drive to the edge of one another
and jump into the unknown,
fantasies we have held dark with one another.

Soft sweater pressed into me smiling wide,
rapidly gaining beat hand arching heat.

I think you found me licking your lips by
accident
as I was listening, there was a moment
and there I was tasting your words.

Roll with me along our sea shore
where we extend each horizon by
a rippling ride of symmetry,
tidal highs wavy lows
and moon windows.

# A COSMIC EXERCISE

They said we could not sculpt
ourselves but we can defy
gravity and shatter
stars, we can shuttle
between time with warm presses
resilient to fading marks.

Tangled possibilities play
between touch points placed
with precision for guided stimulation.

Implausible you say to escape
the ordinary, did you not see
my flash of design—
impatient
recurring
exciting chaos and shine?

# ANGEL

I can't speak for my wandering hands
wanting more of you,
each hunger possessed of you
and where you are leading us tonight.

I can't imagine
the passionate dream weave with certainty—
show me
Angel,
I stand here dripping cherries from the sky.

Petite and freshly laid sun dancing me comatose,
the synth pop perpetrates our simpatico
never dull over this pristine specimen,
a decadent reflection of personality
a violent awakening for me and your lace—
jarring our existence.

A twist of smoke appeared between us
roping together seams
slipping against skin,
shipwrecking our designs.

# CLOUD MANIFESTATIONS

I want to play around fingers
slide between bright gestures
and let tokens from you take me away,
once again—far-far away.

Forever,
let us disappear into the folds
of each other
of this universe
we find beyond the reality that pulls us
each day.

In the end what are we
but circling destiny and rolling chances
watching clouds whisper waves
to another day with you.

At last I have you between stars
and soft dreams
laying out your wonderland
for my eyes to see,
to crawl and to feel again.

# IN EYES OF LIQUID DREAMS

There is a sea so deep yet blue throughout
that I fall fully forward when you look at me.

Along lush canopies we break morning dew,
where sun returns smiles and we waver
just like last night only softer—lighter.

Will you be a wandering soul as am I
when at last I search and step
out into the shadowy world—
fearing broken hearts again?

(I hear your name in my head on my lips
seeing you say my name on your lips
in your head.)

After the brightness of sun and first
looks dimmed we settle into scented corners
rows of us lining the walls, anticipating.

We swim amused in circles
around each other's words doting terms,
for the next few moments
I am the blue of your eyes.

# MAGIC

Stretching boundless in a sea
of wings, wonderings rolling on waves
indecent with exposure,
crossing out stripes and my alibi.

Edges of another night
w/o supple flesh beckoning,
a misty falling wave that conjured itself
upon the incantations of our voodoo love.

Magic is the lunacy between dusk and dawn
dark and right,
the consistent coincidences
putting us on the same train that night.

This fantasy coerces and controls me,
the slightest brush bends me
clear into you leaving me raw—
yet aching for more discipline.

Then it was us streaming,
between steaming shower heads dreaming
of another land placing hands on places
then back again.

# TIDES

As we slipped across the quiet shore
a single wave whispered behind
telling us of a moon dancer—
serene
low
bright at night.

To think of you like the clouds
your sorrow
rain,
and when you beam
the sunlight breathes—
and wind carries us forth.

You, yes you,
on the other side of the world
know that I still love you
even though our lives are opposite,
at least we see the same moon.

When the eyes look w/o deceit
when the fingers breathe w/o thinking,
when your lips become magnetic
with me yes—
willing.

# WE'RE W/O CONSEQUENCE

I softly tread with fingers in bed
gliding over each limb of you,
I strike little sparks that grow
and fold us into a storm.

Let's swim untouchable in a vacuum of leg
rewrapping last night into today,
w/o consequence or care flowing through us.

I taught you to swoon and sigh
after the candle light has passed
and sheets have amassed around while
we dance licking flames of romance,
raging pheromone trains
running off rails sprinting
towards an open chasm.

A silken glance on that face brushed by my hand
touching the regrets of past lovers and a chance,
circling waist lines with beaming
eyes and a black lingerie disguise,
you finger my silvered tongue
proposing to sort the things that come
between us.

# SMOKE SIGNALS

Don't let me be, seize—
the feeling that I left at your shoulder
brushing hair,
sweeping magic as I walked by
those infinite eyes.

My love—
those lashes disguised as lace hide
your true intent I am w/o content
on the outside, let us dive and wonder five senses
release the inner ecstasy let boil time—
hate longing anticipatory,
make flame once again where
emptiness held long before me.

This is no place for modesty—
I assure you,
even empty space has a hard time
escaping our one solid gravitating body
and now—forever, I will find you
from the smoke on the trail you leave,
the fire you breathe drawing me near—always.

# GHOSTS

These are the things
that haunt us.

# THAT

A cool kiss of breeze passes
behind your ear, flows
down neck—blouse,
touches for a brief
moment last night.

Show me your letters each
character ablaze, your
eyes dotting the madness,
is that you on the page
fervently exciting me?

You that firecracker I
hold, watching the fire line
up the gunpowder set
and star bursts ready to
run, blow me and my
hands of you to pieces.

Press glimpses that
poke over at me, that
say things with eyes that
whisper me—near ears that
tell me where we should go tonight.

# SUNRISE & SWITCH

One second
one kiss can change
the pleasure or the pain,
can paint a rainbow over the darkest eyes
of a memory we left behind.

Let the next sunrise splash dew
drops in the morning,
rise to spray orange red blue and purple,
rainbow tails that dry tired eyes.

Let my humidity surround you
as water droplets vibrate encapsulate,
heat and rise—rise to haunt you,
(just think of me).

I never want to reach your (end,
never want to find your toes,
(find the tips of your fingers
because that would mean—(it's all over.

But I will tell you what I like—
if you promise to close) your eyes,
as I kiss you) for the first time)—tonight.

# SCENTFULLY

You couldn't have been a more swirling
static emotional thunder storm
behind those eyes staring me down,
as if through a loaded double barrel.

Let me be where the sea crests your dreams,
where dots poke and pleasure
pushes you over the edge of disaster.

You trigger a silhouette,
I stand nearly free now
w/o disguise eyes glued on the juxtaposition
straddling our tension.

Laced with morning you scent-fully agree
this should continue,
daring the daylight to bend what we have made.

Let every dream haunt me each a finger
of you pressing into another part of my skull,
remember the night we had—we woke up to?

Wishing another day long past due with you—
we may last hiding between curtains
and sheets, sunrises and fancy views.

# S.C.L.A.

Let us weave the light and dark
like phantoms between heaven and hell,
find symmetry in our lustful anger.

Slower I said—so each cellular taste permeates
from hand to mouth to tongue, don't waste
these moments where we synthesize today.

We split—dividing our pulse closer and back
shoving hearts like attacks unsure,
how long we can stay sweet with sweaty flesh?

Bedevil me with those looks that shake
my never ending oscillating eyes,
escalating revolutions that I can't help inside.

If only you left that look on me that
you left last night—today as I wander
now w/o you, wondering if it would be again.

There is only you and I—and this,
what we do to one another
over under between each other,
a smothering coalescent longing ache.

# TELL ME SOMETHING ELSE

Lovingly and suspense baby do me wrong,
take me to the edge of what you know—
placid places simmering with injustice,
tell me how it's done. I know you said to fix
my heart but always will there be a part
of you unseen, a reminder of what was
stitched away—harshly.

We broke the back of the world but
we called it love, it was ours to break—bend
pull—smash and create. What happened to
us in those moments of ours when we were
young and naive (also in love), and
nothing else mattered but us?

It was you waking me in swirling
tongues my hands caught in your hair
and those eyes caught me looking
at you looking at me. I would let your
lightning strike a place in my heart if
only you sensed my static
longing wishing to be struck by you.

# THE WITCH

What is this that wraps and weaves
something arcane for sure,
coming with you and
leaving when
you are gone?

I look for the solitude
for you have lost that chest of longing—
bright feeling to which we both called home.

Let us watch in the morning—
rays how they dance
on our dim skin,
slowly turning breaking moans—
blinding with gusts of wind,
then silent again.

This is my haunting reality—
spiteful tragic dark totality,
your light bends rules as I can see,
breathe through me
touch sincerely
with finality.

# A SPELL FOR ME

If only your whispers
could lead me to sleep
under the willow tree
once again, a supernova
cooling quickly with a slow—
wondrous burn.

You are but a whisper now,
raining on rocks watering down sand,
on a rock somewhere
in the milky way whispering—
hello world. Fingers can whisper too,
like wind in trees along the footsteps
of your arm,
tracing a path toward your eyes.

Let your stir swirl again in circles along
my chest, chase fingertips down to a
carousel spinning round this head,
taste my secrets.

Afterward I shall lay quietly— like
we used to, spent between breaths,
shades, sighs, silent touches that
quiet the soul once more.

# TRANSPARENT TRIALS

Let the fire burn slow tonight,
I hear you like a coarse undertow
with a storming rampant disregard
for conformity,
your seething unrest flows between us.

Let them come and stare
in wonder, grasp their awe
and the concept of what we
nay I—you,
have done to this very instance of time.

Pull the blood
through my heart
when it stops beating
so I can continue to love you,
defying what they believe.

What they said
can be changed simply
through a whisper
or hushed moment,
since now the wind carries all of us.

# LOVE LEFT

She,
the whisper of death,
do I choose my last satisfactions
mortal beings their fixations,
want to see what you taste like in death?

With a flutter,
she waves skirts paving low glows of blush,
a filament bright in her eyes
dissecting what is left of you.

Each snap licks,
tears a piece of streaming reality
until I cry out,
then another repeats blurry
pent up release escapes me.

Will you rage against me and call me your own,
will you show me those depths
where dark breaths escape,
where light becomes lust?

Love left an hour ago when bites found necks
found lips found red nails scratching new
something darker than love—ever knew.

# IMPETUOUS

Soft beating arching bones
and fluttering moans
come home near.

In the night we find the walkers
in stilettos deal half bent,
a fervent need to feel by skylight,
sounds echo and echo and echo.

No need to speak,
let me unbutton and
unfasten your feet,
our pillow top a midnight cloud's delight.

I fall into you w/o thought.

Mention nothing except what you want
say no words carefully poised,
only fingers tongue may speak
you may breathe as loud as you want.

Find me in the places you have forbid yourself—
laced woven and kept safe by mace but,
sometimes behind lips I will not say—
to find me urgently.

# BUT WHEN (AGAIN)

We can play through interludes
as shadow puppets live their alter egos,
secrets that float on tongues
in whispers when you are near,
spaces we close—mouths dear,
remind me again what you are about.

I think we should align on definition,
exactly touch what I need to do
to get that breath from you,
to provide a passionate
unrivaled attention
w/o the playful
chit chat holding us back (in chains).

Will you be my risky decision tonight—
the one I remember when I wake
wondering when again?

# INDEX

# OTHER BOOKS:

Simply You
Only You
Apology

Epiphany
Heart
Lacuna

Calliope
Erato
Thalia

Made in the USA
Middletown, DE
16 January 2023

22234523R00046